TO THE LIMIT
MOTOCROSS

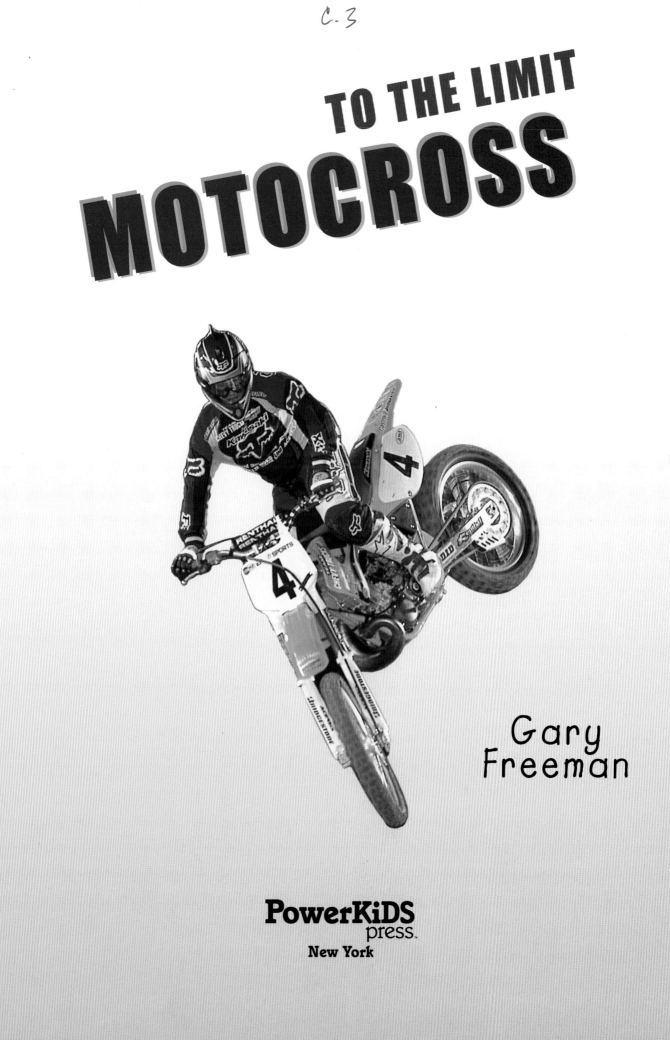

Gary Freeman

PowerKiDS press.
New York

Published in 2012 by the Rosen Publishing Group Inc.
29 East 21st Street, New York, NY 10010

First Edition

Produced for Wayland by Roger Coote Publishing,
Gissing's Farm, Fressingfield, Eye, Suffolk IP21 5SH
Project Management: Mason Editorial Services
Designer: Tim Mayer

Photographs: The publishers would like to thank those who supplied photos for use in this title: all photos by Gary Freeman except pp.6, 7 (top) B.R. Nicholls; pp.11, 23 (top) Frank Hoppen; pp.22, 23 (bottom) Jack Burnicle.

Library of Congress Cataloging-in-Publication Data

Freeman, Gary, 1966–
Motocross / by Gary Freeman. — 1st ed.
        p. cm. — (To the limit)
Includes index.
ISBN 978-1-4488-7027-1 (library binding) — ISBN 978-1-4488-7062-2 (pbk.) — ISBN 978-1-4488-7063-9 (6-pack)
1. Motocross—Juvenile literature. I. Title.
GV1060.12.F74 2012
796.756—dc23
                            2011028823

Manufactured in Malaysia

CPSIA Compliance Information: Batch #WW2012PK: For Further Information contact Rosen Publishing, New York, New York at 1-800-237-9932

CONTENTS

Warning!

Motocross is a dangerous sport. This book is full of advice, but reading it won't keep you safe on the track. Take responsibility for your own safety.

WHAT IS MOTOCROSS?

The start of a race is one of the most exciting moments.

If you're looking for thrills, you've come to the right place: motocross is one of the most exciting sports around. Motocross riders race motorbikes around an outdoor course made of natural obstacles and artificial hazards. The rider who gets around the course quickest is the winner.

All motocross bikes need BIG suspension and knobby tires to cope with the bumps, jumps, and dirt. Racers need to be able to balance on the bike well and control their speed on different parts of the track. Most of all they need a little courage: jumping a motocross bike is very exciting but scary too!

The Secret Language of Motocross

Berm A build-up of earth on the edge of a corner, which lets the riders go around it faster.

Downslope The downward-sloping ramp at the end of a tabletop.

Drop-offs Sheer drops that must be jumped off to continue around the course.

Killer whoops Whoops (see below) but bigger and deeper. Hold on tight!

Moto Another word for "race."

Race line The fastest, most effective route through, over, or past a particular section of track.

Tabletop A jump with a flat top and a ramp at the end.

Whoops A manufactured bumpy section of track. Slow to ride if you get it wrong but spectacular if you get it right.

ROOTS

Motocross has been around for years. In the early days, it was called scrambling. Riders just took their motorcycles off the road and on to rough tracks and hills and scrambled off into the distance. Bikes like the ones racers use today were still a long way off when the first races were held in the 1920s.

As development of bike technology continued so did the riders' skills. The French-based word "motocross" was eventually adopted for the all-new sport. "Moto" is the French word for "motorcycle" and "cross" is an English abbreviation for "cross-country."

Early scramblers take to the tracks.

Photographer Nick Nicholls on Motocross

"In the past you could identify virtually every rider by his clothing and particularly his riding style. You could also see their faces as they rode past. With modern riding gear you can't see the rider's face and there might be three or four on the same track who look exactly the same."

Heroes of the 1960s

Bud Ekins (USA)

Dave Curtis (Britain)

Dick Mann (USA)

Jeff Smith (Britain)

These riders (and their bikes) look a little different, but the thrill is the same.

" It's a totally different sport now from how it was in the past. But in most cases winning came down to rider fitness and that hasn't really changed; you still have to be fit to succeed. "

– Nick Nicholls.

HOW DO THE BIKES WORK?

Motocross and supercross (see pages 10 and 11) bikes are identical. The bikes need high-tech suspension to cope with the extreme conditions. The top speed of a motocross bike is not particularly fast, but its highly tuned engine make acceleration from zero an eye-watering experience.

Silencer (or tailpipe)
Quiets the engine and helps to keep the power flowing smoothly.

Exhaust pipe
Removes waste gas from the engine. Carefully designed to help the engine produce maximum power.

Sprocket and chain Gears are designed for lightning-fast acceleration. Heavy-duty chain drives the power from the engine to the rear wheel.

Swinging Arm
Pivots up and down as the wheel hits the bumps and takes the impact from a big landing.

Almost all motocross bikes have four-stroke engines. These are quieter than the two-strokes that used to be popular, but they are still noisy and smoky. In an effort to improve their bikes, some manufacturers are now working on new fuel-injected engines, where the fuel mixture is controlled by computer.

Throttle
Allows the rider to control speed.

Telescopic Forks
About 12 inches (30 cm) of shock absorption helps ride over bumps.

Radiator
Keeps the engine at the best temperature, which is 212° F (100° C).

Disc Brakes
Powerful disc brakes allow fast braking.

Rear Shock Absorber
About 12 inches (30 cm) of adjustable shock absorption helps soak up the bumps.

Carburetor
Mixes fuel with air as it is sucked into the motor.

SUPERCROSS

Supercross began in the United States, where tracks are constructed inside sports stadiums. Huge tractors use enormous amounts of soil to produce spectacular indoor tracks. The stadium seating gives spectators a bird's-eye view of the tabletop jumps, whoop (and killer whoop) sections, drop-offs, and banked corners. Supercross is one of the most exciting sports on the planet, for racers and the audience alike.

One of the future heroes of the stadiums is James "Bubba" Stewart. Bubba became the AMA Supercross Champion in 2007, at the age of just 22. Unfortunately Bubba then had to sit out the 2008 supercross because of injury (most motocross and supercross riders are badly injured at some point in their career). He was ready to bounce back in 2009, though.

Some supercross races are run in outdoor stadiums.

James "Bubba" Stewart

Birth Date: December 21, 1985

Birthplace: Florida

Lives: Florida

Turned pro: 2002

Bubba is one of the few African Americans to make it to the top in bike racing, which has led to him being called the Tiger Woods of supercross.

Bubba Stewart Selected Highlights

2002: First African-American AMA junior champion

2002: Supercross Rookie of the Year

2004: Won 11 out of 12 races

2006: US Open supercross winner

2007: AMA supercross champion

Powering out of a turn.

TRIALS

Trials riding is the discipline of getting you and your machine over obstacles such as rocks, boulders, tree trunks, and tractor tires. You have to keep your feet on the bike's footpegs (and off the ground). Many of the skills learned on a trials bike are very useful in motocross too. In fact trials riders can usually ride motocross quite well, but the same doesn't always apply the other way around.

The top trials riders are as skillful, controlled, and brave as their motocross buddies but if you're in search of speed, trials might not do it for you. On the other hand, if you want to develop your skill and control on two wheels without the need for speed, trials will be perfect.

> Ride for fun, but think about improving your skill on the bike at the same time. At first you'll probably find it very difficult and you may even fall off, but when you get better you'll be happy that you put in the effort and you'll enjoy yourself much more.
>
> *Adam Raga, top trials rider.*

Trials bikes look very different from motocross bikes.

> **"** If I race an enduro bike against enduro racers, sure they're a bit faster than me. But if they ride a trials bike, they find it impossible to do what I do! **"**
>
> *Adam Raga.*

ENDURO

The mud man cometh!

Enduro is a rough mixture of motocross and trials. It's not as fast as motocross and not as technical as trials, but an enduro rider needs to combine the skills of both sports.

There are several different kinds of enduro racing. In the most common, riders race through woodland areas against the clock. There are special timed sections in which riders have to ride as hard and fast as they can for short bursts, making it an exciting sport to take part in. In other sections, the riders have to get past a series of obstacles as well as they can; any mistakes cost them time.

Hare and Hound (or Hare Scrambles) and cross-country enduro races feature riders racing directly against each other. Unlike motocross, the race lasts for around three hours and riders must refuel at least once during the race.

Enduro Bikes Need:

- Lights.
- License plates.
- Enduro tires.
- Quieter exhaust systems.
- A side stand.

Enduro races can be spectacular.

Differences from Motocross Bikes:

- Geared for better engine response from slow speed.

- Larger fuel tank to cope with the long distances between refuelling stops.

- Hand guards to protect knuckles from trees and branches.

- O-Ring chain uses rubber rings to seal the chain from sand, grit, and dust.

Riding through a water hazard.

❝ Cross-country and Hare Scramble races are like an intense 3-hour motocross. These races are great because you get to spend a long time on the bike and you get to go home feeling really tired! ❞

Paul Edmondson, enduro rider (top picture).

TECHNIQUE 1

This next section takes a quick look at how the professionals ride. Remember, professional riders make it look easy because they practice hard. You'll soon see a big improvement in your own skill on a bike if you do the same.

Starting

Position your weight forward on the bike. Look down at the start gate. Open the throttle to about half. Once the gate drops, let the clutch out quickly but smoothly and introduce full power at the same time. Put both feet on the footpegs as soon as possible.

Braking

Keep your weight back to give the rear wheel as much grip as possible. Downshift as necessary but do not pull in the clutch since you'll lose the braking effect from the engine. Use your judgement to "feel" the tires biting into the dirt.

Corners

Maintain a fast, smooth, and consistent entry speed into the corner. Push your inside foot forward and point your toes to allow the boot to slide on the dirt. As you begin to come out of the corner, introduce more power. Bring your foot back onto the footpeg as soon as possible and return to the standing position while powering away.

TECHNIQUE 2

A good riding technique will not only make you fast, but you'll also look better and in more control. It's best to get it right from the start. Many former racers run schools and academies to show you what to do and why you should do it. A day or more at one of these motocross schools will get anyone's motocross career off to a good start.

Landing jumps safely is an important part of technique.

Jumps

The general rule is to make sure your rear wheel touches the ground just before the front. To achieve this, keep your weight to the rear of the bike on take-off. Make fine adjustments to the flight of the bike in the air by moving your weight either backwards or forwards before landing.

Tabletops

This is the only jump on which you benefit from landing with the front wheel first, but you must be sure to land on the downslope. Take off with your weight back, then in the air move your weight forward. The front wheel will start to drop. Land on the downslope with the front wheel first and introduce the power.

Tabletop landing.

The standing position, shown from behind and in front.

Standing Position

Elbows high, hips over the mid to rear part of the bike. Shoulders just behind the handlebars and head down. Also known as the attack position, this is the correct way to ride aggressively while remaining in control of the bike.

READY TO RACE

Most race meetings are run in a similar way. Racers are divided by age category and engine size, so you usually race against riders of a similar age on similar bikes. Amateur races usually last from 12 to 25 minutes, and there are normally three races in a day. Each lap of the course lasts between 1.5 and 3 minutes. Track marshals will be overlooking every part of the course.

No two tracks are the same: practicing and racing on lots of different surfaces will help you become a better rider.

Race-Day Tips

- Always walk the track before the race and learn its features.

- Watch the other races (particularly the start) and familiarize yourself with the format.

- Make friends with as many other riders as possible and never be afraid to ask for advice. Race meetings and clubs are rider-friendly hangouts.

Race-Day Jargon Buster

Holding area – Where bikes and riders wait before going to the start gate.

Start gate – A metal gate that drops to start the race (it usually drops towards the riders).

Paddock – The place where competitors park their cars and bikes.

Scrutineering – The safety checking of all bikes at the beginning of the race meeting by race officials. Items that are checked include: wheel bearings, brakes, suspension, spokes, sprockets, chain, tires, levers, helmet, and riding gear.

Practice – Free practice at the beginning of the race meeting, usually only for a few laps.

TOP DOGS

Let's take a quick look at two of the most dominant riders of the sport's past.

Dave Thorpe

Dave won seven professional British Motocross titles and three 500cc World Championships, making him the most successful British motocross rider ever. His speed and strength on the huge 500cc bikes was an amazing sight.

Dave Thorpe Fact File

250cc British Champion 1982

500cc British Champion 1983, 1984, 1985, 1986, 1987, 1989

500cc World Champion 1985, 1986, 1989

Ricky Carmichael celebrates his first "perfect" (unbeaten) season.

Ricky Carmichael Fact File

AMA motocross champion 2000, 2001, 2002, 2003, 2004, 2005, 2006

AMA supercross champion 2001, 2002, 2003, 2005, 2006

First-ever "perfect" seasons, in 2002 and 2004

Ricky Carmichael

Ricky Carmichael is probably the greatest motocross and supercross rider ever. In fact, his nickname is "Goat," which stands for "Greatest of All Time." By the time he retired in 2007, Ricky had won more than 100 top-level races, far more than any other rider. He had also finished two perfect seasons, in which he won every motocross race.

Dave Thorpe, the most successful British rider ever, controls his 500cc bike in the air.

SAFETY FIRST

Motocross is a dangerous, high-speed sport, and accidents can happen. The best way of minimizing the risk of being hurt if you're in an accident is to wear the right gear. But the best way to avoid being in an accident at all is to ride within your limits. If you feel that you no longer have complete control of the bike or your speed, ease off: otherwise you'll be a danger to yourself and other racers.

It's better to take a smoother line (left) than lose control (below).

Helmet

Goggles

Body Armor
(under race shirt)

Race Shirt

The fastest and most successful riders make riding and winning look easy by maintaining their control and composure on the bike. If in doubt, choose the smoother race line and slow down: the chances are it'll be faster anyway.

The last, most important safety advice is never, ever ride alone. If something happens to you, there will be no one there to get help.

Gloves

Race Pants

Knee Pads

Motocross Boots

FIT TO RIDE

You don't really have to be strong to race motocross, but you do need to be fit. Racing motocross is all about controlled aggression over the period of the race. Amateur races last from 12 to 25 minutes, but professionals can race for up to 45 minutes and, at full speed, motocross is one of the hardest sports you'll ever try. Being fit gives you the edge you need to do well and at the same time, you'll enjoy the racing more.

No one muscle group necessarily needs to be stronger than the other but the ones that get the most punishment are the:

- Lower back
- Thighs
- Shoulders
- Neck

Try these sports to improve and maintain your fitness:
- Running
- Swimming
- Biking
- Aerobics
- Soccer

Fitness Food
What's Hot
What's Not

What's Hot	What's Not
Rice	Candy
Pasta	Chips
Potatoes (not french fries)	Cheese
Fruit and vegetables	Chocolate
Water	Soft drinks
Chicken and fish	Red meat
Whole-grain cereals	Sugar-coated cereals

ETHICS AND QUIZ

Quiz Time

1 **You're approaching a tabletop jump and you take off perfectly. Where is the best landing place?**

a) On top of the tabletop, then ride off the end.

b) On the downslope with the front wheel first.

c) On the level track after the obstacle.

2 **While riding at an official practice track, you see someone in front riding very slowly. What do you do?**

a) Shout so they know to move over.

b) Give them lots of room and ride past gently.

c) Race past and show them how it's done.

3 **The carburetor on a motocross bike does what?**

a) Holds the rear wheel in place and pivots up and down as the wheel hits the bumps.

b) Mixes the fuel with air as it is sucked into the motor.

c) Keeps the engine at optimum temperature.

Unofficial motocross tracks are usually found in remote, otherwise peaceful areas. These unofficial tracks give motocross a bad name and make it harder for new, official tracks to be built. Most makeshift tracks aren't really worth the time and effort. There are no bathrooms, no first aid, and no snack truck. Riding at official tracks, where you may end up racing one day, will help you improve faster and it's also much safer.

How Did You Do?

Mostly a) – Well done, you've achieved the almost impossible by being 100% wrong. Start reading the book again from the beginning and this time turn off the TV.

Mostly b) – Hey, top score. You're a quick learner.

Mostly c) – You're OK but there's room for improvement. As long as you didn't answer question 2) with answer C, you'll be fine.

Practice-Track Ethics

- If you see someone fall, go and help. Get them and their bike off the track as fast as possible.

- Join and exit the track at the designated point and nowhere else.

- Ride the track only in the official direction.

- Give slower riders a wide berth. You were learning once, too.

- BE FRIENDLY to people and never forget that motocross is fun!

GLOSSARY

bars (BAHRZ) Short for "handlebars."

carb (KAHRB) Short for "carburetor," the thing that mixes fuel and air together.

forks (FORKS) Front suspension, which soaks up bumps as the bike goes across rough ground.

grips (GRIPS) Handlebar hand grips, which help the rider grip the handlebars.

jet (JET) The internal part of a carburetor that controls fuel flow.

pegs (PEGZ) Foot pegs, on which the rider's feet rest.

pipe (PYP) Exhaust pipe, which takes waste gas out of the engine.

pivot (PIH-vut) Point around which something moves in a circular motion.

plug (PLUG) Spark plug, which ignites fuel in the engine to provide power.

shocks (SHOKS) Rear suspension, which soaks up bumps as the bike goes across rough ground.

tailpipe (TAYL-pyp) Exhaust silencer, which keeps the exhaust from being too noisy.

throttle (THRAH-tul) Twist grip to control the engine speed.

Books

Agratin, Dario. *Off Road Champions.* Woodland Parks, CO: Book-Em.

Martin, Michael. *Ricky Carmichael: Motorcross Champion.* Mankato, MN: Capstone Press, 2004.

McGrath, Jeremy. *Wide Open: A Life in Supercross.* New York: Harper Colins, 2004.

Web Sites

Due to the changing nature of Internet links, PowerKids Press has developed an online list of Web sites related to the subject of this book. This site is updated regularly. Please use this link to access the list:
www.powerkidslinks.com/limit/moto/

INDEX

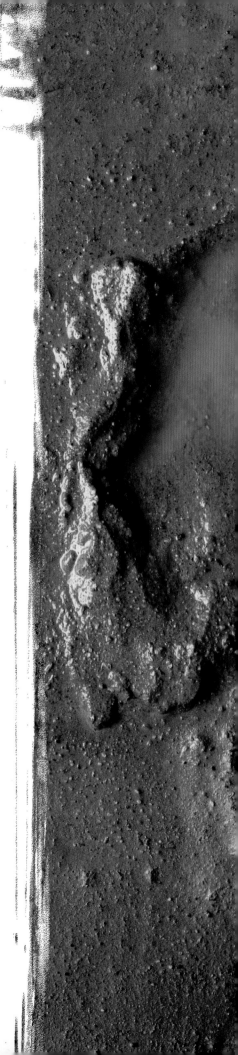